# Contents

Some call him Captain Fantastic, some call him Captain Cool. Fans and players call him Boo Boo but his real name is Mark Alleyne. He is Captain of Gloucestershire County Cricket Club – the most successful side ever in one-day cricket.

Mark with the NatWest Trophy, Benson & Hedges Cup and Benson & Hedges Super Cup

# Record-breaking Gloucestershire

1st August 1999 Benson & Hedges Super Cup
beat Yorkshire by 124 runs at Lords

29th August 1999 NatWest Trophy
beat Somerset by 50 runs at Lords

10th June 2000 Benson & Hedges Cup
beat Glamorgan by 7 wickets at Lords

28th August 2000 NatWest Trophy
beat Warwickshire by 22 runs at Lords

2000 Norwich Union Trophy
finished top of the division

Kings of One-Day Cricket

Alleyne and co. book place in record books

Four in a row for the Lords

# Growing Up

Mark was born in London on May 23rd 1968 and then he moved to Barbados in 1972. "I spent 11 years growing up in Barbados where everyone was cricket mad – if you didn't play cricket you were weird!" By the time he was eight, Mark was playing cricket for his school.

When he was 15, Mark came back to England. "I found my first year back in England difficult. But being good at sport (I played football and basketball as well as cricket) helped me to fit in and make friends."

"I loved school. Apart from playing cricket it was where my friends were. Maths and science were my favourite subjects. I thought I would have a job which would use maths in some way – an accountant, for example.

I always wanted to play cricket but I didn't think it would be my job! I thought I would play cricket and do something else as well.

When I came back to England I played for Middlesex Colts and started to follow county cricket. That's when I knew I wanted to be a professional cricketer."

# Playing for GCCC

Mark with a model of W G Grace in the GCCC Education Centre

Gloucestershire County Cricket Club has had many famous players but the most famous of all was Dr W G Grace. He was born in 1848 and died in 1915. He was an all-rounder who scored 126 centuries in first class cricket – the first when he was 18 and the last when he was 56!

Mark Alleyne joined Gloucestershire County Cricket Club in 1986. Mark's elder brother Stephen was with the club for a short while and he had the nickname 'Yogi'. So when Mark arrived, younger and smaller than his brother, he just had to be called 'Boo Boo'!

Mark with a model of himself in the GCCC Education Centre

Mark is an all-rounder. He is good at batting, bowling and fielding. He says: "I love doing all three but I get more satisfaction from doing well in batting. I'm more of a support bowler but if I bat well I make a big contribution to the team. When I'm batting I can just concentrate on that, but when we're fielding I have to concentrate on getting the right guys in the right places. As captain, I have to think about everyone's job not just my own."

# Career Milestones

| | |
|---|---|
| *1986* | **Became the youngest player ever to score a century for Gloucestershire** |
| *1988* | **Became a regular first team player** |
| *1990* | **Became the youngest ever double centurion for Gloucestershire when he scored 256 against Northants** |
| *1997* | **Became Captain of GCCC** |
| *1999* | **Scored 112 runs in the Benson & Hedges Super Cup final and was voted Man of the Match**<br>**First played for England's one-day side** |

The Benson & Hedges Super Cup

Mark with his Benson & Hedges winner's medals

**2000** Captain of England A team tour to Bangladesh
and New Zealand
Judged best batsman of the tour and given
£1000 from the tour sponsors
Named as a Wisden Cricketer of the Year

**2001** Captain of England A team tour to West Indies
and Sri Lanka

# Life as a
## Professional Crickete

Mark was extra busy in his Benefit Year. Lots of things were done to raise money for him – including selling teddy bears!

The cricket season starts in April but the players work hard before that on pre-season training. Gloucestershire players go on a pre-season tour to South Africa so they can play matches in warm weather.

In a typical week during the season players will:

- play one four-day game

- play a one-day game

- spend several hours travelling

- have one day for training and recovery. The amount of recovery depends on a player's work load. Bowlers may have had a heavy day so they need more recovery time.

- go to team meetings.

Mark says that if he is lucky, he may get half a day off a week. He also says that if rain didn't stop them from playing sometimes, players probably wouldn't get through the whole season!

# Training and Fitness

Players train to keep fit and practise their skills. Training sessions start with a short team game like football to warm players up.

Players have to warm up on match days too. "We need to fire our muscles ready for action and improve elasticity. We do a lot of stretches – the kinds of movements you make when playing. We do this as a group about one and a half hours before the match.

Warming up at the County Ground, Bristol

Working hard in the gym!

After playing, the team needs to warm down so that their muscles can recover quickly for the next day's play. During the day the muscles contract and build up lactic acid. Stretching gets rid of this.

"Some players have an ice bath and then a warm shower. I don't! I have a fifteen-minute slow jog and stretch. This is also my quiet thinking time when I go over what we've done well, what we could do better and what we'll do tomorrow."

# Clothes and Equipment

Gloucestershire players have two different strips. They wear blue for the one-day Norwich Union games. They wear white for all the other matches. The club provides all the clothes but players do their own washing!

Mark wearing the blue strip, with a team mascot and Lancashire Captain, John Crawley

The players' normal white strip

Mark says, "I usually take four pairs of trousers and six shirts to away games. Some clubs have laundry rooms for players to wash their whites if they need to. When it comes to socks, I seem to have millions of them all over the house. My wife, Louise, wears them in the winter!"

Mark takes at least three bats to a match – often more. "I get through three or four bats in a season. About 95% of the time I use a bat that weighs 2 lb 10 oz, but I need a lighter bat if I'm facing a fast bowler – I can move it faster!"

Mark talking to the author about his bat

Cricket bats are made of willow and the closer the grain of wood, then the better a bat is. A bat costs about £250. Clubs do not provide equipment so each player has to find his own sponsor. The sponsor provides all the equipment – bats, boots, pads and so on. Different sponsors also provide cars for the players.

# Match Days

**Do you get nervous before a match?**

"Yes all the time, but I've never felt so nervous that I've lost confidence. It's more the adrenaline rush that you need to play well. Waiting to bat gives you little butterflies. Lots of guys find that as soon as they put on their pads they want to go to the loo!"

**What do you do when it's raining and you are waiting to play?**

"Players chat, play cards, do crossword puzzles – that kind of thing. It's a chance to catch up on some paperwork, so I tend to leave my match reports for rainy days.

We don't have a huge amount of time to practise during the season because of the heavy fixture list, so wet days give us the chance to train and top up our skills."

"My bit of the dressing room!"

**Which is the match you will always remember and why?**

"There are two. The first final we played at Lords was special. The excitement builds as you get through each stage of a competition and there is a great sense of occasion playing in a Lord's final.

The other match was my England debut against Australia in Brisbane. That was more nerve-racking because you are trying to prove yourself when you play for your country for the first time."

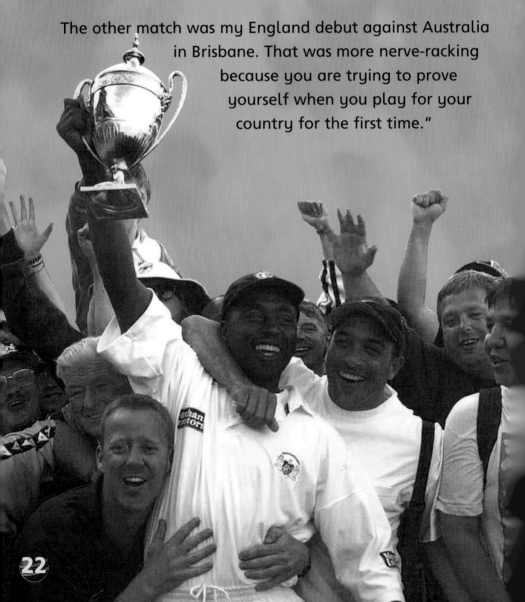

Mark with one of his England caps and shirts

Mark has played for England ten times so far. He was in his car when he found out that he had been picked for the England one-day squad to go to Australia. He was driving home after the Benson & Hedges Super Cup Final when he heard it on the radio. He pulled in to a motorway service station and rang his mother-in-law. He got her to check on teletext to make sure he hadn't misheard it on the radio!

# Captain Fantastic

Mark Alleyne is one of the best County Captains. Jack
Russell, Gloucestershire's famous wicket keeper who
played for England many times says: "He's always in the
thick of the action … he has one of the smartest 'cricket
brains' I know."

As the captain, Mark has to lead the side during matches and make decisions about where to place the fielders, who should bowl and so on. But a lot of the captain's work takes place off the field. He works with the coach, John Bracewell, to select the team. He also has to support the rest of the players and encourages everyone to take part and make suggestions in team meetings. "I want them all to feel part of the group, we have a very strong team bond."

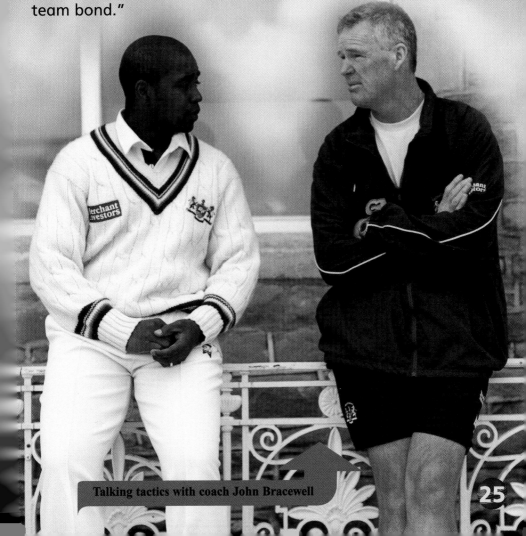

Talking tactics with coach John Bracewell

As captain, Mark also:

- takes care of the day-to-day running of the cricket side of the club with the coach – training and so on

- writes a match report after every game about the umpires and the pitch

- represents the club when rules of cricket or things which affect players are being reviewed and discussed

- gives TV, radio and newspaper interviews

- gives talks to groups who are interested in cricket.

Mark with the Lord Mayor of Bristol when the city celebrated the team's success

Another interview for Mark!

# Some Final Questions

**What is the average length of playing career for a professional cricketer?**

"About 15 years. You usually get a contract at 19 or 20 and finish in your mid thirties."

**Do you know what you would like to do when you finish playing?**

"Most players want to stay in the game – in the business side of clubs, umpiring, coaching or whatever – but there aren't enough jobs for all of them. I want to go into business and apply what I've learned from sport."

**What's the most exciting thing that's happened in your career?**

"There have been different milestones – getting into the first team, scoring my first century, the Lords finals, playing for England ... if you want to play for England you know you have to work your way up to it, so anything that took me a step closer was exciting."

Yet another autograph to sign!

Mark's bowling figures in the 1999 NatWest Trophy final at Lords

**ALLEYNE**

| OVERS | 10 |
|---|---|
| MAIDENS | 0 |
| RUNS | 37 |
| WICKETS | 3 |
| WIDES | 0 |
| NO BALLS | 0 |

## What do you like least about being a professional cricketer?

"The motorway travelling in between games – especially when I'm driving back after a long day and I'm tired. I do about 14,000 miles a year. We don't always take our own cars – we share. We have a kit van which takes all our things to matches for us."

## What do you like best about being a professional cricketer?

"I just love playing cricket – it's what makes it easier to get up in the morning!"

Captain Fantastic and the One-Day Kings!

# Index